ZIPPY
CHOOSES A SPORT

by Carla Golembe

For Barbara Kern, who loves to play tennis

One day Zippy sees that he has a big tummy. He is getting fat.
"I need some exercise," he thinks.

Zippy goes to the basketball *court.

*為生字，請參照生字表

He picks up the ball and *throws it at the *hoop. But Zippy is very short and the hoop is very high. He can not get the ball through the hoop. "Maybe I'll try baseball," he says.

Zippy goes to the park. He brings his baseball and *bat.

He stands at *home plate with his bat. But there is nobody to throw the ball to him. So he has to play baseball *alone.

He throws the baseball in the air and tries to hit it with the bat.
He hits himself on the nose.

"Ouch!" *yells Zippy. "Maybe I'll try bowling."

8

Zippy goes to the Sports *Equipment store.

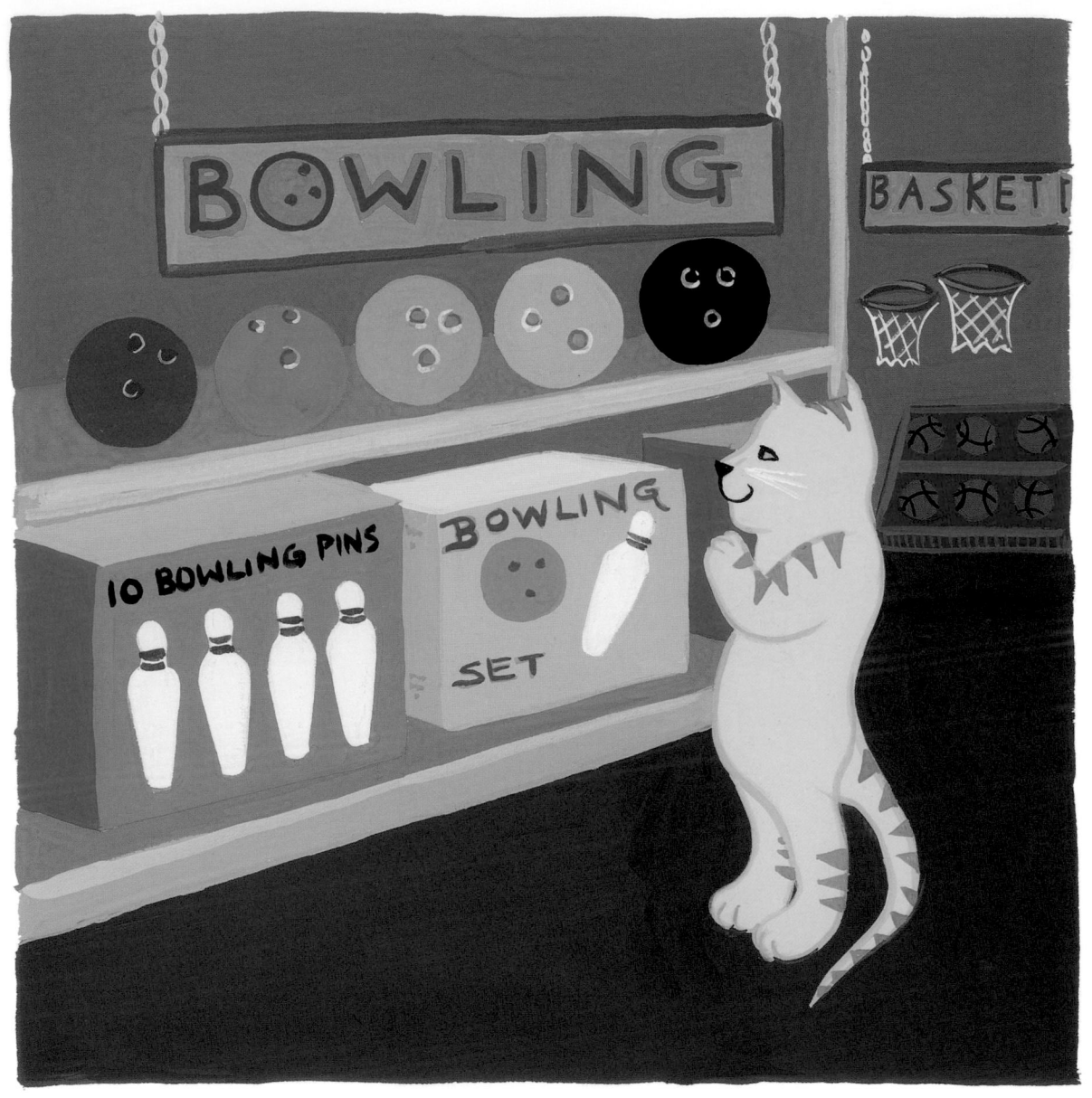

He sees bowling balls in many colors. There are red balls, blue balls, pink balls, and green balls. They are really big.

Zippy picks up the blue ball. It is so heavy that he drops it on his toe.

"Ouch!" yells Zippy. "Maybe I'll ride a bicycle."

Zippy buys a bicycle. He rides it down the street.
"This is fun," he says.

But then his tail gets caught in the wheel.
"Ouch!" cries Zippy as he jumps off the bicycle.

Then Zippy sees Zoe walking down the street.
She is carrying two *tennis rackets.

"There you are," says Zoe. "Will you play tennis with me?"

So Zippy and Zoe play tennis. And Zippy is so happy.
The net is not too high and Zippy can hit the ball over it.

Zoe loves to play tennis so Zippy has someone to play with.
The ball is just the right size.

17

Zippy holds his tail away from the racket when he runs.

Now Zippy and Zoe play tennis every day. Zippy does not have a big tummy anymore. He is *nice and thin.

賽皮做運動

🎾 **p.3**

有一天，賽皮發現自己有個大大的肚子。
他變胖了。
他想：「我要做些運動才行。」

🎾 **p.4**

賽皮跑去籃球場。

🎾 **p.5**

他撿起籃球，對著籃框投籃。但是賽皮的個子很矮，而籃框的位置很高，所以他沒辦法把球投進籃框裡。
他說：「我還是試試看棒球好了。」

🎾 **p.6**

賽皮到公園去。他還帶著他的棒球和球棒。

p.7

他拿著球棒站在本壘板上，可是沒有人投球給他，所以他只好自己一個人打。

p.8

他把球拋向空中，試著用球棒打它，結果卻打到了自己的鼻子。

賽皮大叫：「好痛喔！也許我該試試保齡球。」

p.9

賽皮跑到運動用品專賣店。

p.10

他看到許多不同顏色的保齡球：有紅色、藍色、粉紅色和綠色，這些球都很大。

p.11

賽皮拿起藍色的球，結果它太重了，賽皮沒有抓好，不小心把球砸在腳趾上。

賽皮大叫：「好痛喔！也許我該試試騎腳踏車。」

p.12

賽皮買了一輛腳踏車。
他在街道上騎著它。
賽皮說：「好好玩喔！」

p.13

但接著他的尾巴就被輪子夾住了。
賽皮從腳踏車上跳下來，大叫著：「好痛喔！」

p.14

這時，賽皮看到柔依走在街上，她帶著兩支網球拍。

p.15

柔依說：「你在這裡啊！想不想跟我一起打網球呢？」

p.16
所以，賽皮和柔依就一起去打網球。賽皮好高興喔！
球網不會太高，所以賽皮打的球可以越過球網。

p.17
柔依喜歡打網球，所以賽皮有一起打球的對象。
而網球的尺寸也剛剛好。

p.18
當賽皮在跑的時候，都讓尾巴離網球拍遠遠的。

p.19
現在，賽皮和柔依每天都打網球。賽皮再也沒有大大的肚子了。他不但變得很瘦，

p.20
而且還玩得很開心呢！

我愛做運動

Part. 1

肚子變胖的賽皮在故事中嘗試了許多運動，你對這些運動認識了多少呢？趕快來測試一下吧！

（正確答案在第28頁喔！）

(a)　(b)　(c)　(d)　(e)

(f)　(g)　(h)　(i)

1 Zippy goes to play ___basketball___ . He needs ___(a)___ and _____ .

2 Zippy goes to play _____ . He needs ___(c)___ and ___(d)___ .

3 Zippy goes to play ___tennis___ . He needs _____ and _____ .

4 Zippy goes to play ___bowling___ . He needs _____ and _____ .

5 Zippy goes to ride a ___bicycle___ . He needs _____ .

Part. 2

小朋友，你平常有沒有養成良好的運動習慣呢？下面就讓我們來檢視一下你的運動狀況吧！

🔍 我的運動大檢視

姓名：＿＿＿＿＿＿＿＿＿＿＿＿　　年齡：＿＿＿＿＿歲

身高：＿＿＿＿＿公分　　體重：＿＿＿＿＿公斤

我的理想體重是：＿＿＿＿＿公斤

註：理想體重(以公斤為單位) = 22×身高^2(以公尺為單位)
　　實際體重應介於理想體重的 ±10% 之間
　　你可以請家長幫忙計算自己的理想體重

我平均每週運動＿＿＿＿＿次，每次運動＿＿＿＿＿分鐘。

我最喜歡的運動：1.＿＿＿＿＿　　2.＿＿＿＿＿　　3.＿＿＿＿＿

我最討厭的運動：1.＿＿＿＿＿　　2.＿＿＿＿＿　　3.＿＿＿＿＿

體能小測試：

1. 仰臥起坐 30 秒，我能做幾下？＿＿＿＿＿下

請加強	還可以	正常	不錯	好厲害 →
0	6	9	14	16

2. 立定跳遠，我能夠跳幾公分？＿＿＿＿＿公分

請加強	還可以	正常	不錯	好厲害 →
0	80	90	125	135

活(ㄏㄨㄛˊ)動(ㄉㄨㄥˋ)解(ㄐㄧㄝˇ)答(ㄉㄚˊ) ：

1. (h)　　　　2. baseball　　　3. (e), (i)

4. (b), (g)　　5. (f)

Author's Note

There is nothing true about this story. I made everything up. I wanted to write a story about Zippy that has something to do with sports. But all the other sports seemed to be too difficult for him. It seems like tennis is the best sport for Zippy.

作者的話

這則故事是我想像出來的，並不是真實的故事。我想寫一篇和賽皮與做運動有關的故事，但是其他的運動，對他來說好像都太難了。對賽皮來說，網球似乎是最適合他的運動呢！

29

❧ About the Author

Carla Golembe is the illustrator of thirteen children's books, five of which she wrote. Carla has won several awards including a New York Times Best Illustrated Picture Book Award. She has also received illustration awards from Parents' Choice and the American Folklore Society. She has twenty-five years of college teaching experience and, for the last thirteen years, has given speaker presentations and workshops to elementary schools. She lives in Southeast Florida, with her husband Joe and her cats Zippy and Zoe.

❧ 關於作者

Carla Golembe 擔任過十三本童書的繪者，其中五本是由她寫作的。Carla 曾多次獲獎，包括《紐約時報》最佳圖畫書獎。她也曾獲全美父母首選基金會，以及美國民俗學會的插畫獎項。她有二十五年的大學教學經驗，而在過去的十三年中，曾經在多所小學中演講及舉辦研討會。她目前和丈夫 Joe 以及她的貓——賽皮與柔依，住在美國佛羅里達州東南部。

賽皮與柔依系列

ZIPPY AND ZOE SERIES

想知道我們發生了什麼驚奇又爆笑的事嗎？
歡迎學習英文0-2年的小朋友一起來分享我們的故事 ──
「賽皮與柔依系列」，讓你在一連串有趣的事情中學英文！

精裝／附中英雙語朗讀CD／全套六本

Carla Golembe 著／繪
本局編輯部 譯

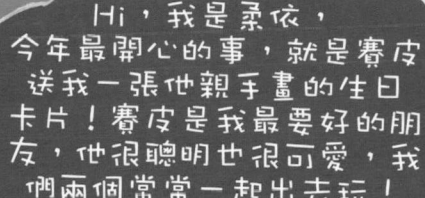

Hello！我是賽皮，我喜歡畫畫、做餅乾，還有跟柔依一起去海邊玩。偷偷告訴你們一個秘密：我在馬戲團表演過喔！

Hi，我是柔依，今年最開心的事，就是賽皮送我一張他親手畫的生日卡片！賽皮是我最要好的朋友，他很聰明也很可愛，我們兩個常常一起出去玩！

賽皮與柔依系列有：

1 賽皮與綠色顏料
(Zippy and the Green Paint)
2 賽皮與馬戲團
(Zippy and the Circus)
3 賽皮與超級大餅乾
(Zippy and the Very Big Cookie)
4 賽皮做運動
(Zippy Chooses a Sport)
5 賽皮學認字
(Zippy Reads)
6 賽皮與柔依去海邊
(Zippy and Zoe Go to the Beach)

I Love My Family Series

我愛我的家 系列

Kathleen R. Seaton　著／姚紅　繪

附中英雙語朗讀 CD

適讀對象：學習英文 0～2 年者（國小 1～3 年級適讀）

六本全新創作的中英雙語繪本，
六個溫馨幽默的故事，
帶領小朋友們進入單純可愛的小班的生活，
跟他一起分享和家人之間親密的感情！

國家圖書館出版品預行編目資料

Zippy Chooses a Sport:賽皮做運動 / Carla
Golembe著;Carla Golembe繪;本局編輯部譯. —
—初版一刷. ——臺北市：三民，2006
　　面；　　公分. ——(Fun心讀雙語叢書.賽皮與柔
　　依系列)
中英對照
ISBN 957–14–4453–7　（精裝）

1. 英國語言－讀本

523.38　　　　　　　　　　　　94026567

網路書店位址　http://www.sanmin.com.tw

©　Zippy Chooses a Sport
——賽皮做運動

著作人	Carla Golembe
繪　者	Carla Golembe
譯　者	本局編輯部
發行人	劉振強
著作財產權人	三民書局股份有限公司 臺北市復興北路386號
發行所	三民書局股份有限公司 地址／臺北市復興北路386號 電話／(02)25006600 郵撥／0009998–5
印刷所	三民書局股份有限公司
門市部	復北店／臺北市復興北路386號 重南店／臺北市重慶南路一段61號

初版一刷　2006年1月
編　號　S 806201
定　價　新臺幣壹佰捌拾元整
行政院新聞局登記證局版臺業字第○二○○號

有著作權‧不准侵害

ISBN　957–14–4453–7　（精裝）